Count on

Count and draw the hops. Writ

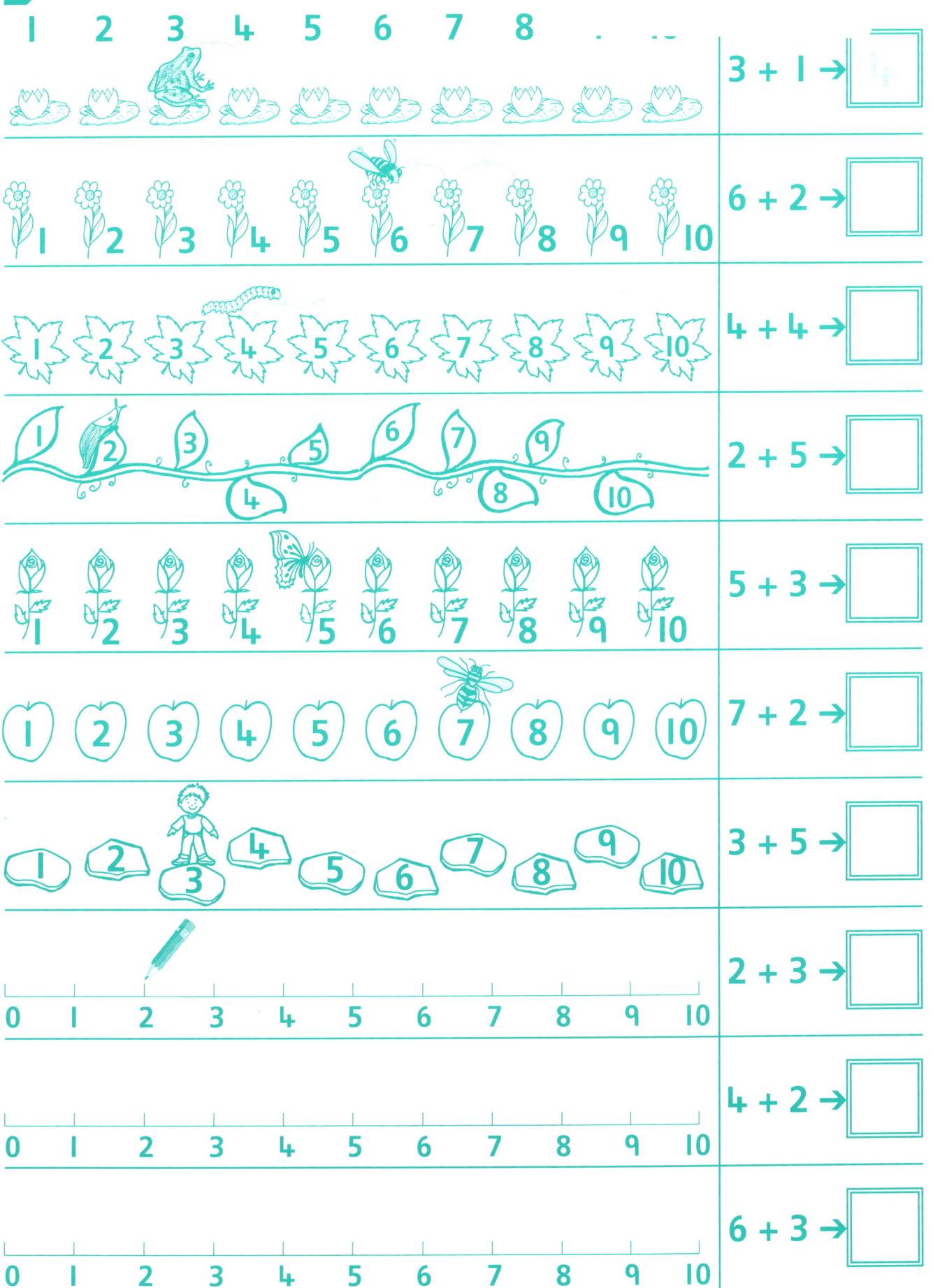

1 2 3 4 5 6 7 8 9 10	3 + 1 → 4
1 2 3 4 5 6 7 8 9 10	6 + 2 →
1 2 3 4 5 6 7 8 9 10	4 + 4 →
1 2 3 4 5 6 7 8 9 10	2 + 5 →
1 2 3 4 5 6 7 8 9 10	5 + 3 →
1 2 3 4 5 6 7 8 9 10	7 + 2 →
1 2 3 4 5 6 7 8 9 10	3 + 5 →
0 1 2 3 4 5 6 7 8 9 10	2 + 3 →
0 1 2 3 4 5 6 7 8 9 10	4 + 2 →
0 1 2 3 4 5 6 7 8 9 10	6 + 3 →

▶ Colour the bigger number.

| 4 6 | 2 9 | 3 7 | 4 1 |
| 8 6 | 5 7 | 2 1 | 9 3 |

▶ Colour the smaller number.

| 2 7 | 1 4 | 6 3 | 2 9 |
| 4 8 | 5 3 | 2 3 | 10 5 |

▶ Fill in the missing numbers.

_ _ _ _ _ _ 7 8 9 10

▶ Write the number after:

| 3 | | | 8 | | | 5 | | | 7 | | | 1 | |
| 6 | | | 4 | | | 9 | | | 0 | | | 2 | |

▶ Write the number before:

| | 7 | | | 2 | | | 10 | | | 3 | | | 1 |
| | 4 | | | 9 | | | 6 | | | 8 | | | 5 |

▶ On the caterpillar, colour the numbers before 8 and after 4.

4

Find the difference

▶ Who has more? Colour the difference.

Jo
Kiran

Who has more?
Kiran
has [1] more.

Sam
Preda

Who has more?
[ ]
has [ ] more.

Debjani
Ivan

Who has more?
[ ]
has [ ] more.

Lisa
Tom

Who has more?
[ ]
has [ ] more.

Jip
Spot

Who has more?
[ ]
has [ ] more.

Flossie
Tiddles

Who has more?
[ ]
has [ ] more.

Bob
Peter

Who has more?
[ ]
has [ ] more.

▶ Write a number greater than

7 [ ]   5 [ ]   6 [ ]

▶ Write a number less than

6 [ ]   8 [ ]   2 [ ]

5

Counting back

▶ Write the number.

8 − 2 → 6

5 − 4 → ☐

Write down the missing numbers.

10
9
8
4

7 − 4 → ☐   10 − 6 → ☐   6 − 2 → ☐   9 − 7 → ☐

4 − 3 → ☐   9 − 3 → ☐

▶ Count back   8 − 5 → ☐   ▶ Count back   5 − 2 → ☐

0 1 2 3 4 5 6 7 8 9 10   0 1 2 3 4 5 6 7 8 9 10

▶ Write the number 2 less than 6. ☐   ▶ Write the number 4 less than 5. ☐

6

Money

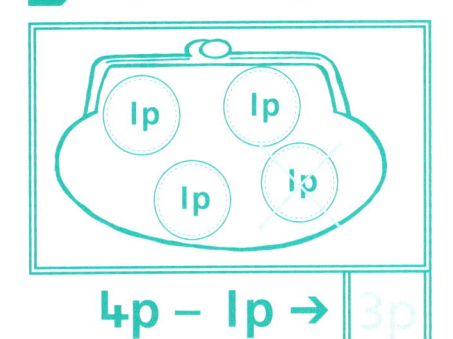

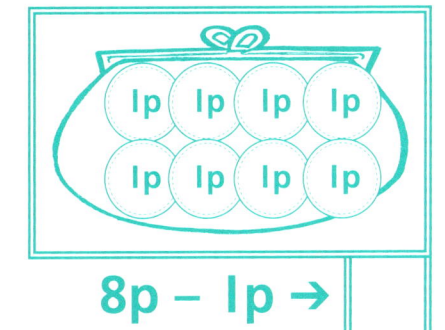

▶ **Spend 1p. Take 1p away.**

4p − 1p → 3p

8p − 1p →

10p − 1p →

▶ **Spend 4p. Take 4p away.**

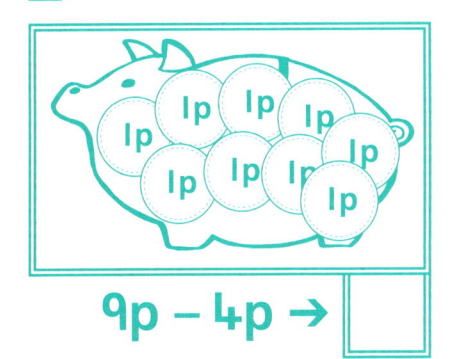

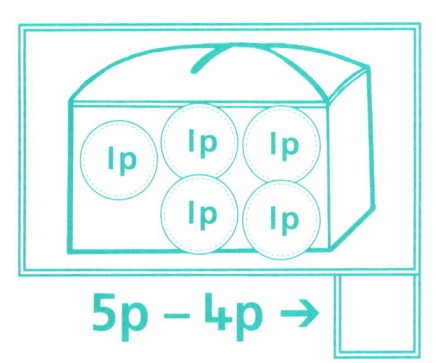

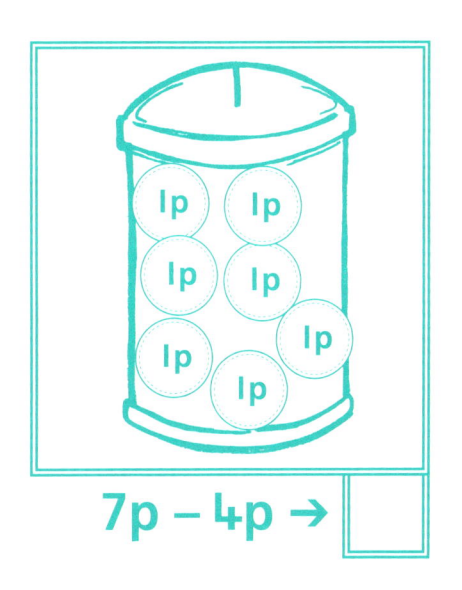

9p − 4p →

5p − 4p →

7p − 4p →

▶ **Colour the pile with the least money in it.**

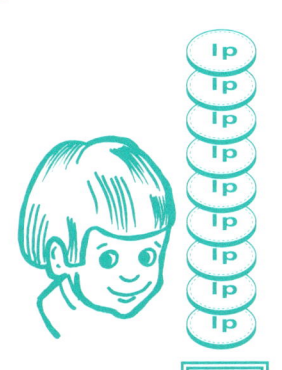

Emma ☐ p   Jonah ☐ p   Jack ☐ p   Kerry ☐ p

Who has least money?

Who has most money?

7

Find the difference

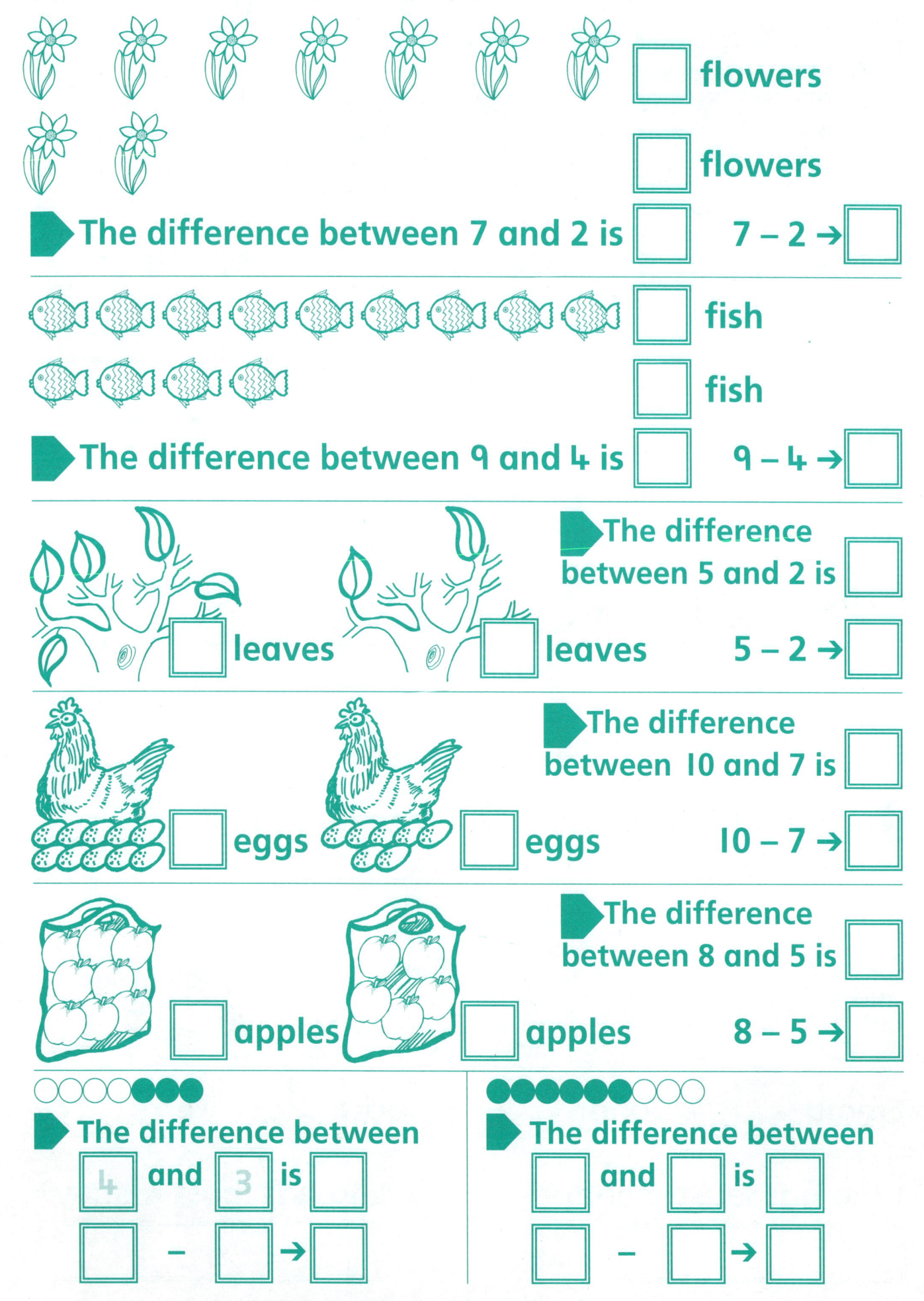

☐ flowers

☐ flowers

▶ The difference between 7 and 2 is ☐   7 − 2 → ☐

☐ fish

☐ fish

▶ The difference between 9 and 4 is ☐   9 − 4 → ☐

☐ leaves   ☐ leaves

▶ The difference between 5 and 2 is ☐

5 − 2 → ☐

☐ eggs   ☐ eggs

▶ The difference between 10 and 7 is ☐

10 − 7 → ☐

☐ apples   ☐ apples

▶ The difference between 8 and 5 is ☐

8 − 5 → ☐

▶ The difference between 4 and 3 is ☐

☐ − ☐ → ☐

▶ The difference between ☐ and ☐ is ☐

☐ − ☐ → ☐

Number Families

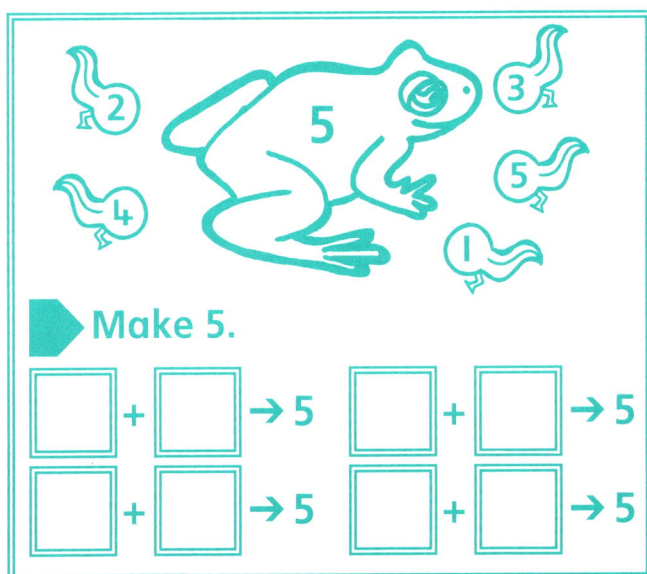

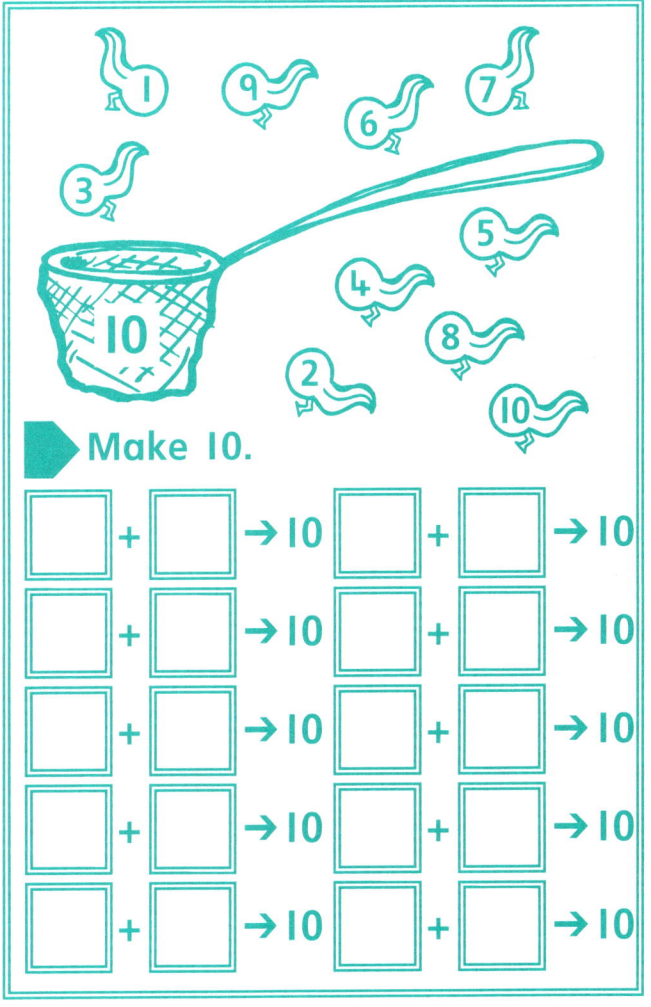

Join the tadpoles to make 7. Write the sum.

6	+	1	→ 7	☐ + ☐	→ 7
4	+	3	→ 7	☐ + ☐	→ 7
☐	+	☐	→ 7	☐ + ☐	→ 7

Make 5.

☐ + ☐ → 5   ☐ + ☐ → 5
☐ + ☐ → 5   ☐ + ☐ → 5

Make 4.

☐ + ☐ → 4
☐ + ☐ → 4
☐ + ☐ → 4

Make 9.

☐ + ☐ → 9   ☐ + ☐ → 9
☐ + ☐ → 9   ☐ + ☐ → 9
☐ + ☐ → 9   ☐ + ☐ → 9
☐ + ☐ → 9   ☐ + ☐ → 9

Make 10.

☐ + ☐ → 10   ☐ + ☐ → 10
☐ + ☐ → 10   ☐ + ☐ → 10
☐ + ☐ → 10   ☐ + ☐ → 10
☐ + ☐ → 10   ☐ + ☐ → 10
☐ + ☐ → 10   ☐ + ☐ → 10

Solve the problem

5	ducklings
3	ducklings walk away
2	ducklings left

5 − 3 → 2

	birds
	birds fly away
	birds left

☐ − ☐ → ☐

	apples
	apples fall off
	apples left

☐ − ☐ → ☐

	puppies
	puppies run away
	puppies left

☐ − ☐ → ☐

	piglets
	piglets playing
	piglets left

☐ − ☐ → ☐

	squirrels
	squirrels leaping
	squirrels left

☐ − ☐ → ☐

How long?

▶ Draw round your foot and cut out the shape.
Use the shape to measure with.
Estimate first. Then measure.

Measure	Estimate	Measure with your foot shape
table	☐ feet	☐ feet
tray unit	☐ feet	☐ feet
chair	☐ feet	☐ feet
door	☐ feet	☐ feet
sand tray	☐ feet	☐ feet

▶ Now draw round your hand and cut out the shape. Use the shape to measure with.

Measure	Estimate	Measure with your hand shape
window	☐ hands	☐ hands
bookcase	☐ hands	☐ hands
cupboard	☐ hands	☐ hands
sink	☐ hands	☐ hands
cushion	☐ hands	☐ hands

▶ Compare your results with your friends' results.

How long?

▶ Estimate first.
Then measure with a paper-clip and a straw.

	Estimate	Measure	Estimate	Measure
book	☐ paper-clips	☐ paper-clips	☐ straws	☐ straws
shoe	☐ paper-clips	☐ paper-clips	☐ straws	☐ straws
paintbrush	☐ paper-clips	☐ paper-clips	☐ straws	☐ straws
10 cubes	☐ paper-clips	☐ paper-clips	☐ straws	☐ straws
felt tip	☐ paper-clips	☐ paper-clips	☐ straws	☐ straws

▶ Now measure with a crayon and with 10 cubes joined together.

	Estimate	Measure	Estimate	Measure
wastebin	☐ crayons	☐ crayons	☐ cubes	☐ cubes
box	☐ crayons	☐ crayons	☐ cubes	☐ cubes
jigsaw	☐ crayons	☐ crayons	☐ cubes	☐ cubes
chair	☐ crayons	☐ crayons	☐ cubes	☐ cubes
ruler	☐ crayons	☐ crayons	☐ cubes	☐ cubes

▶ Compare your results with your friends' results.

Time

▶ Colour the hands on the clocks.
Use red for the hour hand and blue for the minute hand.
▶ Complete the time in the box.

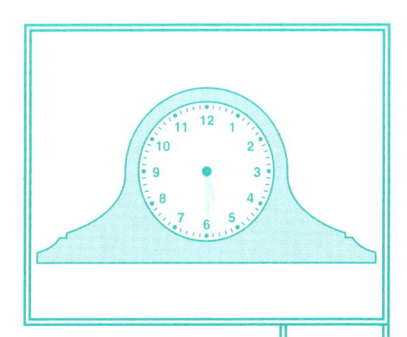

½ past 2

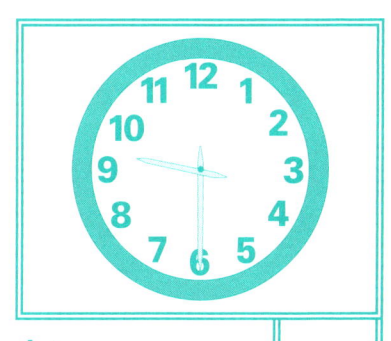

½ past

½ past

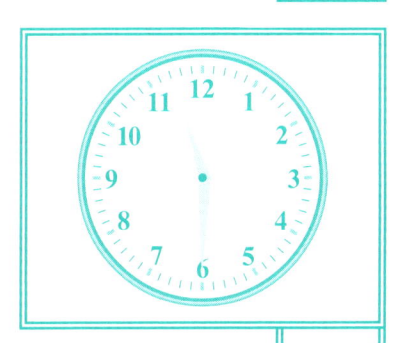

½ past

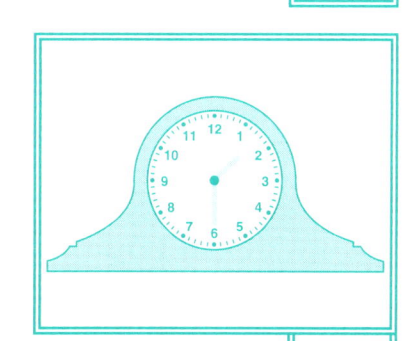

½ past

½ past

½ past

½ past

½ past

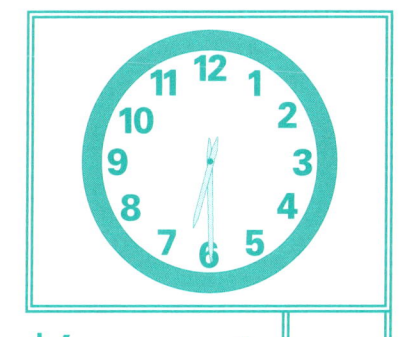

½ past

½ past

½ past

13

Time

▶ Draw the hands on the clocks.
Use red for the hour hand and blue for the minute hand.

½ past 4

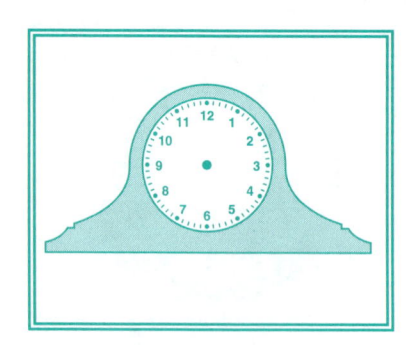

½ past 1

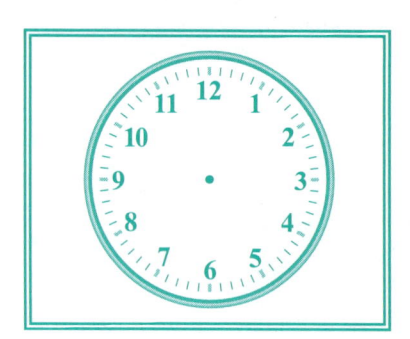

½ past 10

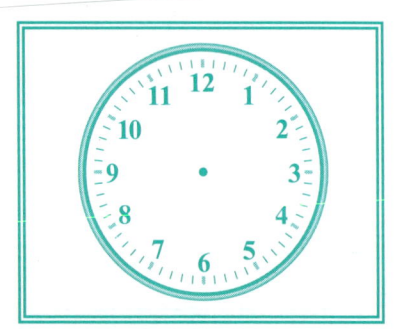

½ past 7

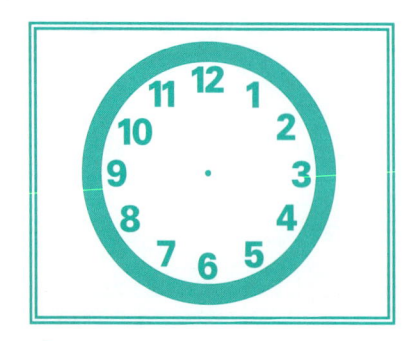

½ past 8

½ past 3

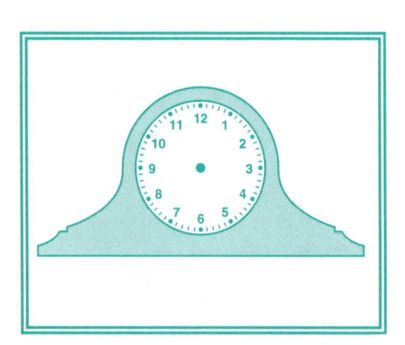

½ past 5

½ past 12

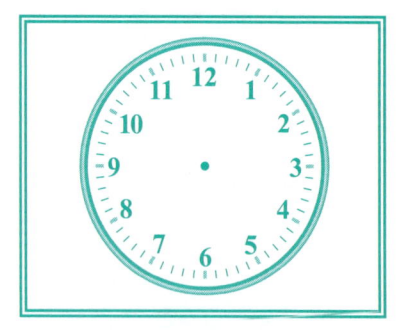

½ past 2

½ past 6

½ past 9

½ past 11

14

All take aways

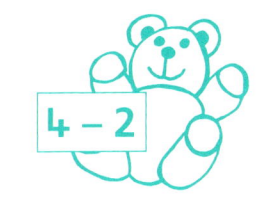

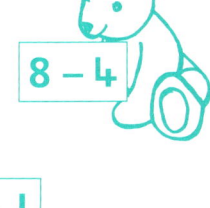

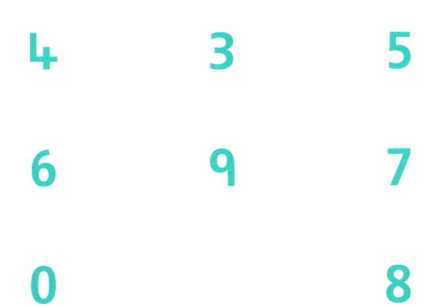

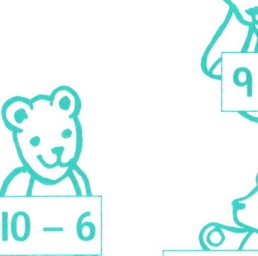

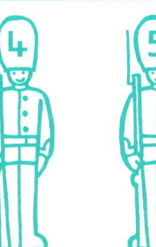

▶ Match to find the answer.

1	10	2
4	3	5
6	9	7
0		8

4 − 2
8 − 4
2 − 1
10 − 0
7 − 1
9 − 6
5 − 5
9 − 9
10 − 6
10 − 5
9 − 2
9 − 1

▶ Use the soldiers to help you answer the sums.

9 − 5 → ☐   8 − 6 → ☐   7 − 2 → ☐
6 − 3 → ☐   10 − 3 → ☐   4 − 2 → ☐
4 − 1 → ☐   5 − 1 → ☐   8 − 0 → ☐
10 − 8 → ☐   9 − 3 → ☐   10 − 6 → ☐
7 − 4 → ☐   6 − 2 → ☐   9 − 7 → ☐

▶ Write the number before:

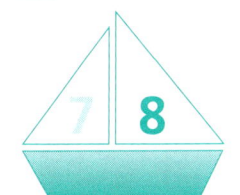

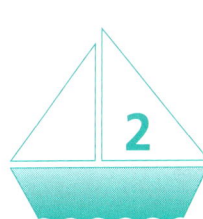

7 | 8   ☐ | 4   ☐ | 7   ☐ | 9   ☐ | 2   ☐ | 10

Add and take

▶ Colour the fish if the answer is 5.

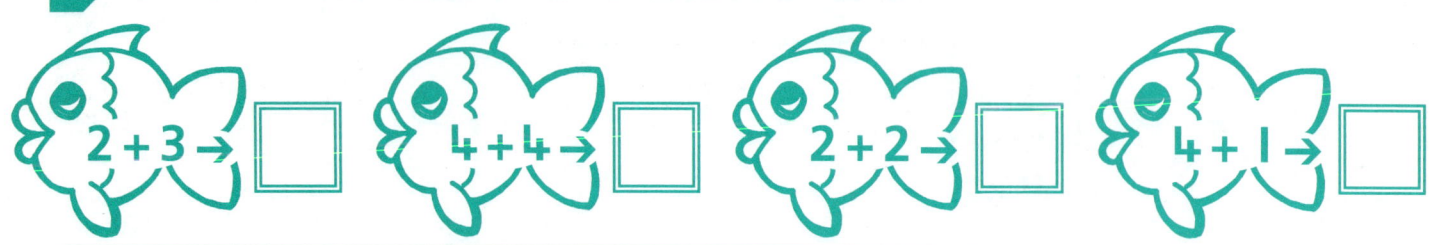

2 + 3 → ☐   4 + 4 → ☐   2 + 2 → ☐   4 + 1 → ☐

▶ Colour the shell if the answer is 3.

10 − 7 → ☐   8 − 5 → ☐   9 − 2 → ☐   8 − 4 → ☐

▶ Colour the boat if the answer is 9.

5 + 2 → ☐   4 + 5 → ☐   6 + 1 → ☐   7 + 2 → ☐

▶ Colour the sandcastle if the answer is 6.

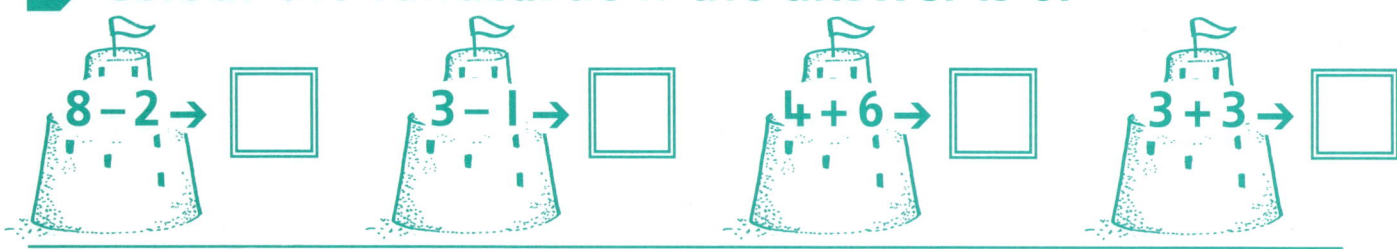

8 − 2 → ☐   3 − 1 → ☐   4 + 6 → ☐   3 + 3 → ☐

▶ Colour the flag if the answer is 8.

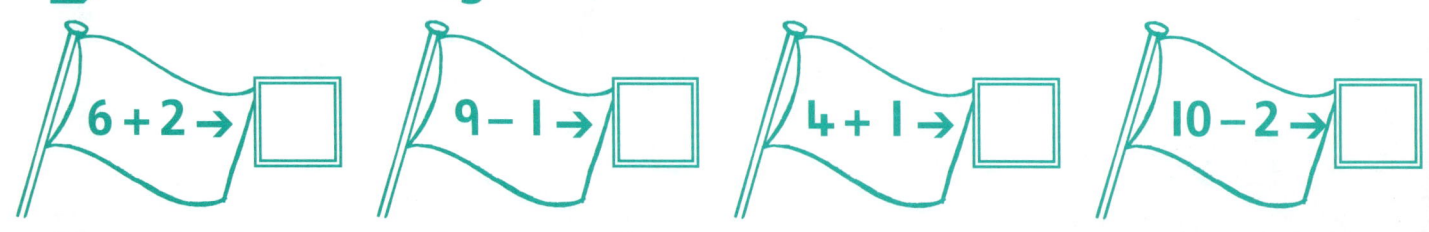

6 + 2 → ☐   9 − 1 → ☐   4 + 1 → ☐   10 − 2 → ☐

▶ Colour the shark if the answer is 4.

8 − 2 → ☐   4 + 0 → ☐   6 − 2 → ☐   5 + 3 → ☐

Count back.

6 − 4 → 2
9 − 2 →
2 − 1 →
8 − 4 →
3 − 2 →

10 − 8 →
6 − 2 →
4 − 3 →
5 − 0 →
1 − 1 →

7 − 4 →
2 − 0 →
6 − 5 →
9 − 7 →
5 − 4 →

5 − 2 → 3
7 − 2 →
10 − 6 →
7 − 5 →
9 − 3 →

7 − 1 →
10 − 3 →
8 − 1 →
4 − 0 →
6 − 3 →

8 − 5 →
3 − 3 →
10 − 7 →
1 − 0 →
2 − 2 →

5 − 3 → 2
2 − □ → 1
8 − □ → 5
9 − □ → 7
7 − □ → 6

10 − □ → 9
8 − □ → 6
4 − □ → 2
5 − □ → 3
9 − □ → 6

7 − □ → 4
3 − □ → 1
6 − □ → 2
10 − □ → 6
6 − □ → 3

Solve the problem

3 balls in the air.
5 balls on the ground.
8 balls altogether.

3 + 5 → ☐

☐ clowns altogether.
☐ clowns driving off.
☐ clowns left behind.

☐ − ☐ → ☐

☐ clowns altogether.
☐ on the wire.
☐ on the ground.

☐ − ☐ → ☐

☐ women.
☐ men.
☐ people altogether.

☐ + ☐ → ☐

☐ men on the ground.
☐ men standing on shoulders.
☐ men altogether.

☐ + ☐ → ☐

☐ clowns altogether.
☐ clowns on the elephant.
☐ clowns on the ground.

☐ − ☐ → ☐

Money

▶ How much have the children saved?

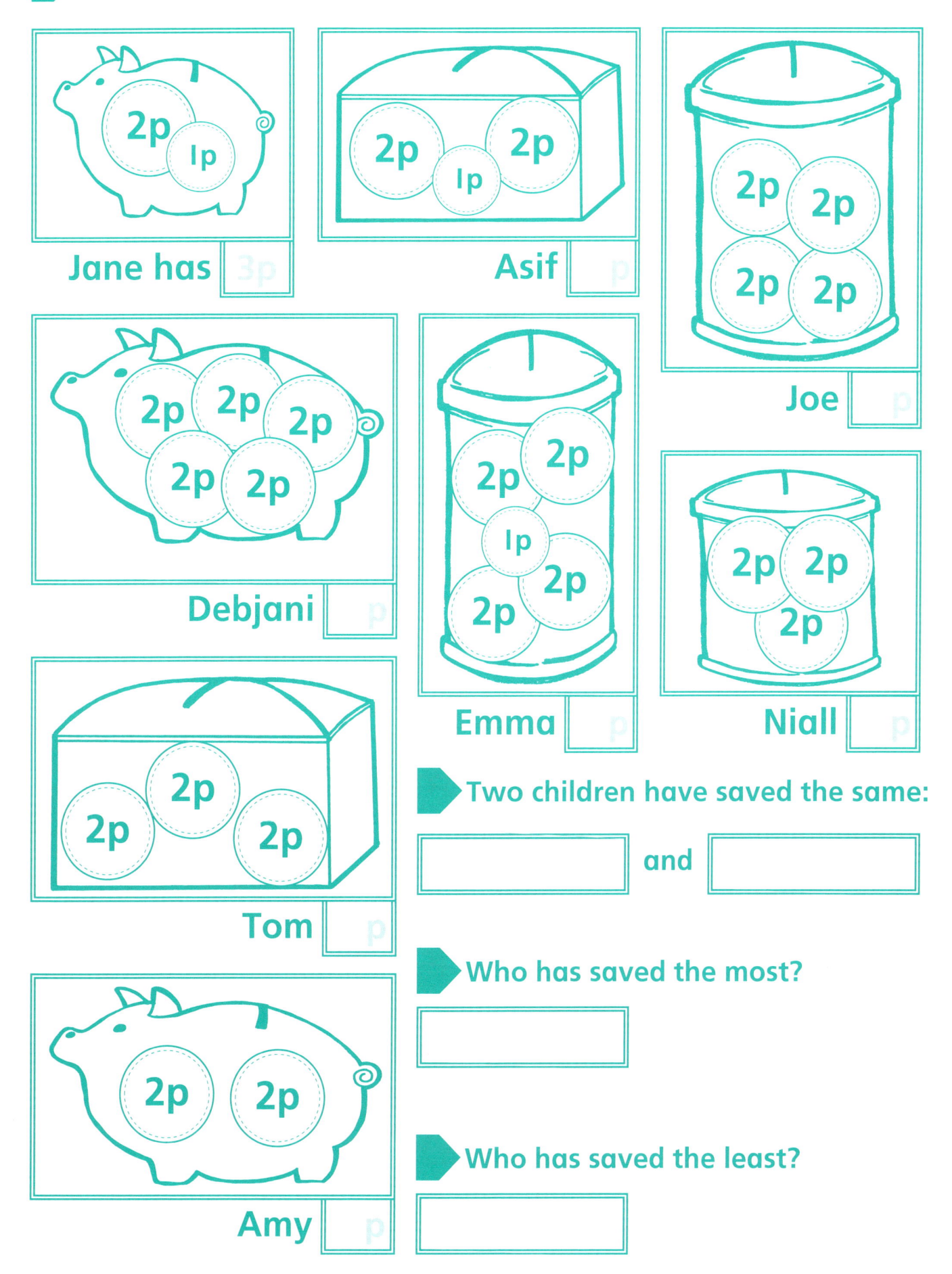

Jane has 3p

Asif ___ p (5p)

Joe ___ p (8p)

Debjani ___ p (10p)

Emma ___ p (9p)

Niall ___ p (6p)

Tom ___ p (6p)

Amy ___ p (4p)

▶ Two children have saved the same:

___ and ___

▶ Who has saved the most?

___

▶ Who has saved the least?

___

▶ **Draw the coins in the purses.**
Use 2p (2p) and 1p (1p) coins.

4p • 3p • 8p • 7p • 10p • 6p • 1p • 9p • 2p • 5p

20

What have you spent?

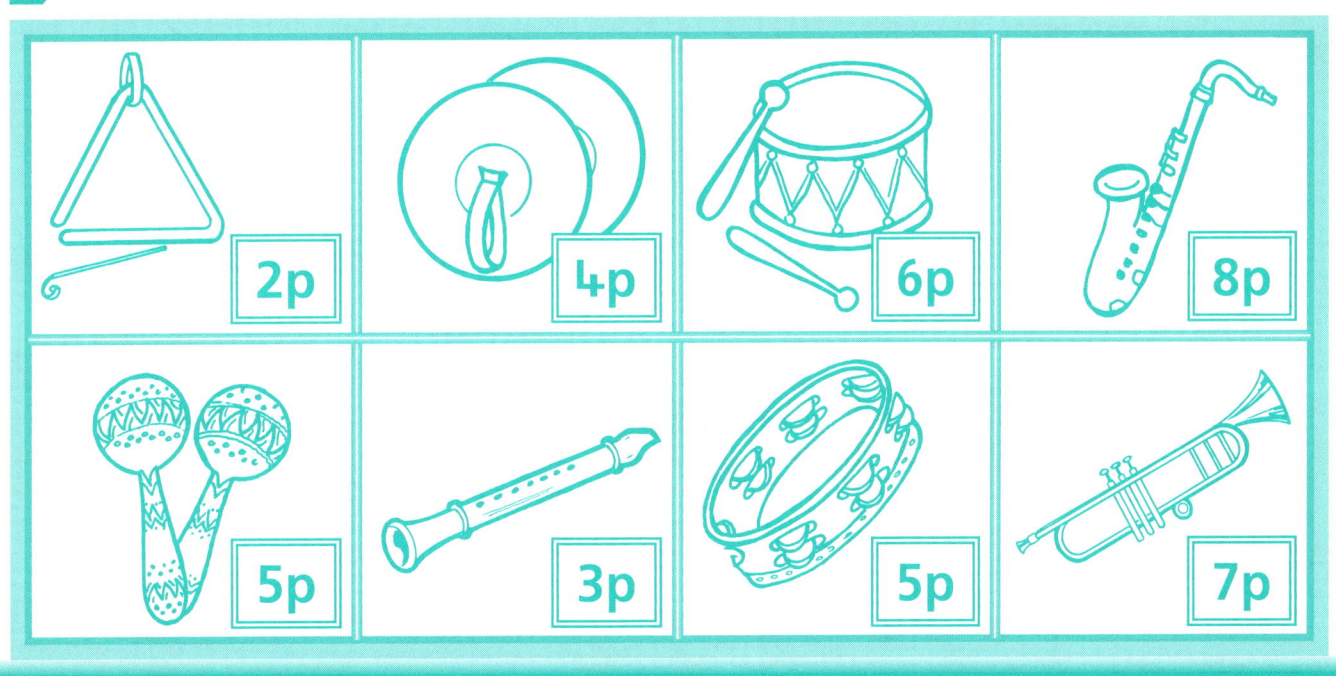

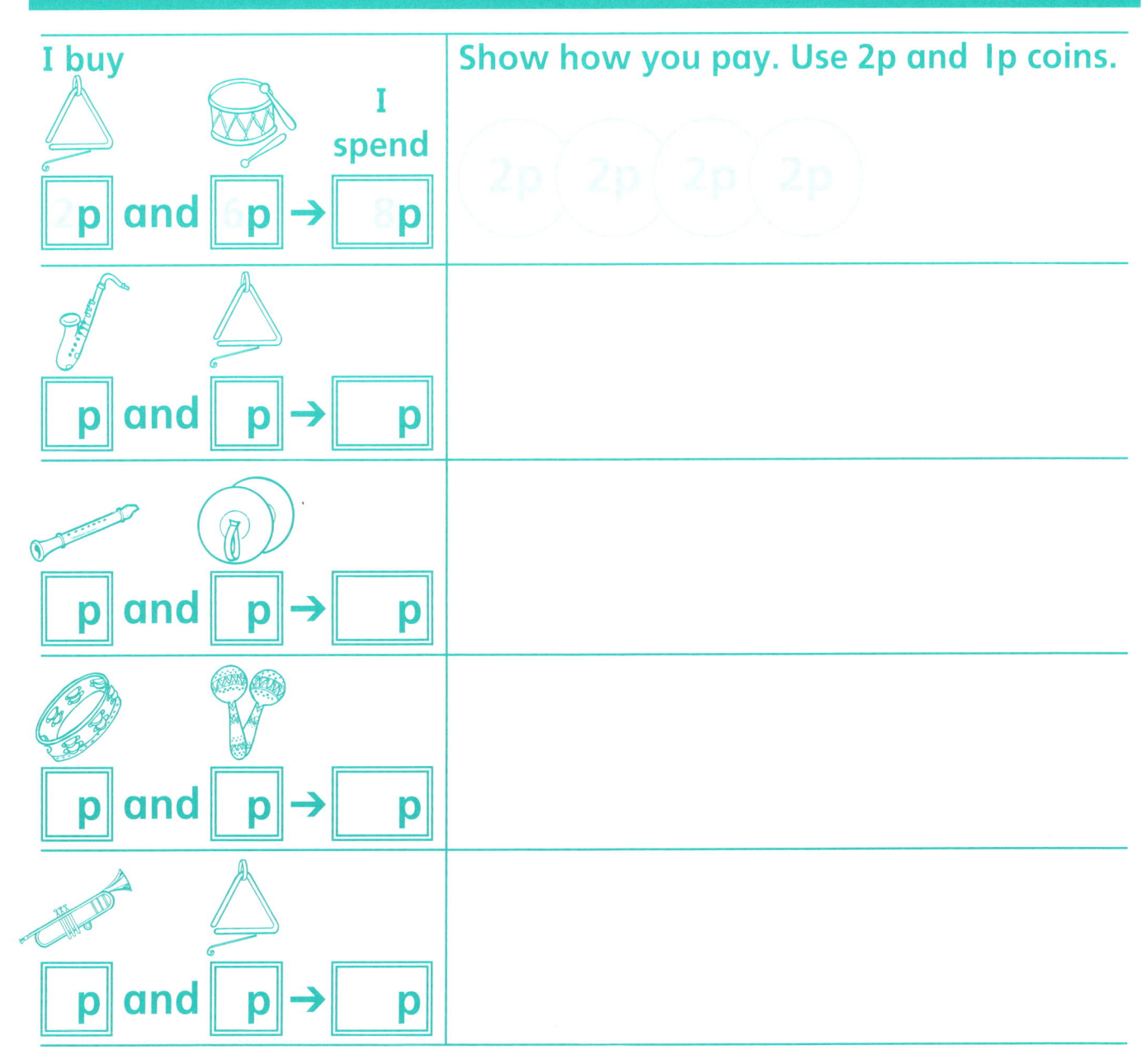

triangle 2p	cymbals 4p	drum 6p	saxophone 8p
maracas 5p	recorder 3p	tambourine 5p	trumpet 7p

I buy — triangle and drum — **I spend**

2p and 6p → 8p

Show how you pay. Use 2p and 1p coins.

2p 2p 2p 2p

saxophone and triangle

☐p and ☐p → ☐p

recorder and cymbals

☐p and ☐p → ☐p

tambourine and maracas

☐p and ☐p → ☐p

trumpet and triangle

☐p and ☐p → ☐p

▶ Match the coins to the pictures.

4p 3p 5p
7p 6p 8p
9p 10p

▶ Draw how much change you need.

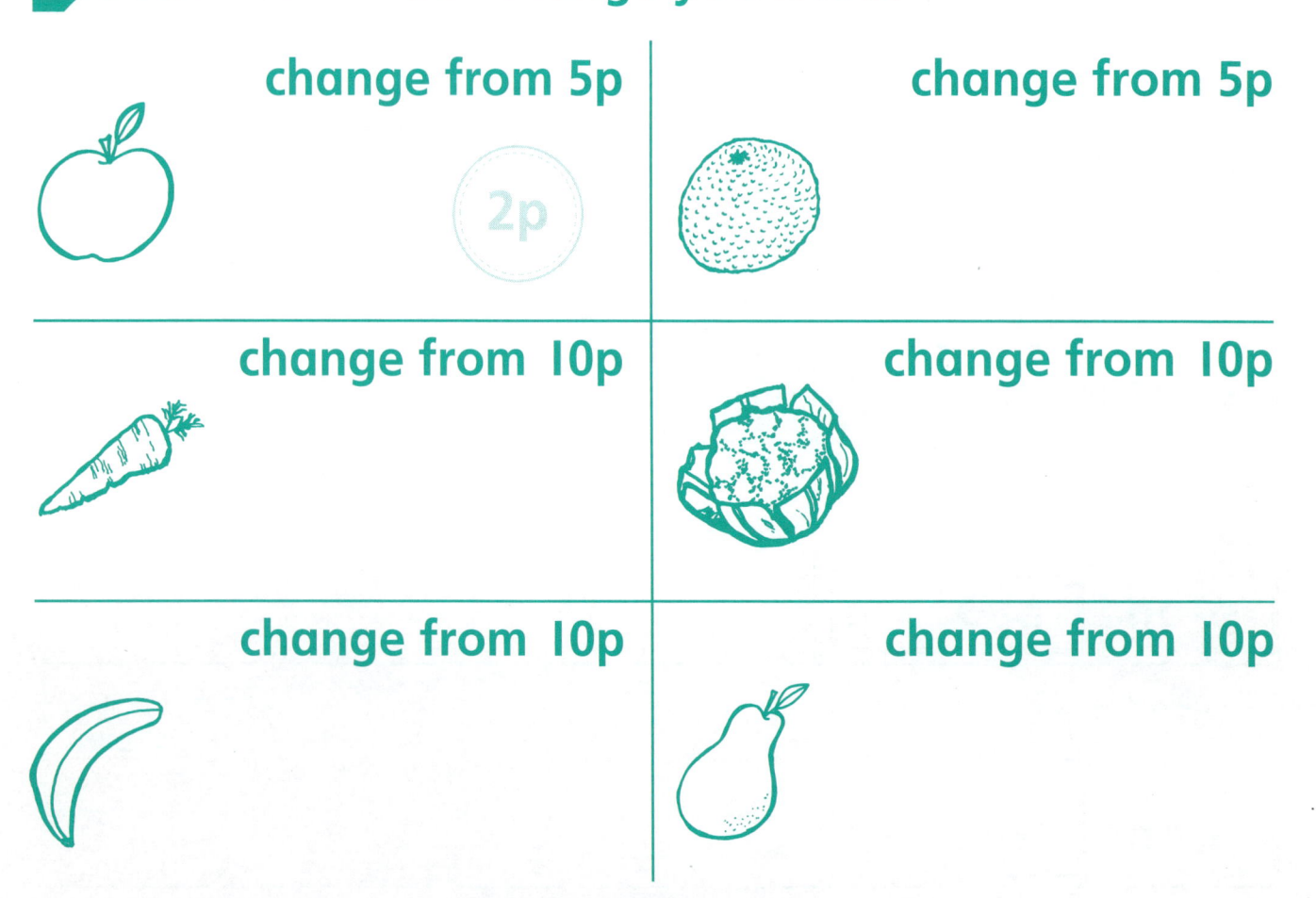

change from 5p   2p   change from 5p

change from 10p   change from 10p

change from 10p   change from 10p

22

Weighing

Weigh 4 of these	Use Marbles		Use Shells	
	Estimate	Weight	Estimate	Weight
conkers	☐ marbles	☐ marbles	☐ shells	☐ shells
fir-cones	☐ marbles	☐ marbles	☐ shells	☐ shells
pencils	☐ marbles	☐ marbles	☐ shells	☐ shells
cubes	☐ marbles	☐ marbles	☐ shells	☐ shells
crayons	☐ marbles	☐ marbles	☐ shells	☐ shells
pebbles	☐ marbles	☐ marbles	☐ shells	☐ shells
paintbrushes	☐ marbles	☐ marbles	☐ shells	☐ shells
glue spreaders	☐ marbles	☐ marbles	☐ shells	☐ shells
nails	☐ marbles	☐ marbles	☐ shells	☐ shells
toy cars	☐ marbles	☐ marbles	☐ shells	☐ shells
scoops of sand	☐ marbles	☐ marbles	☐ shells	☐ shells

▶ **Discuss your results with your friends.**

Weighing

▶ Make the pans balance. Estimate first, then balance.

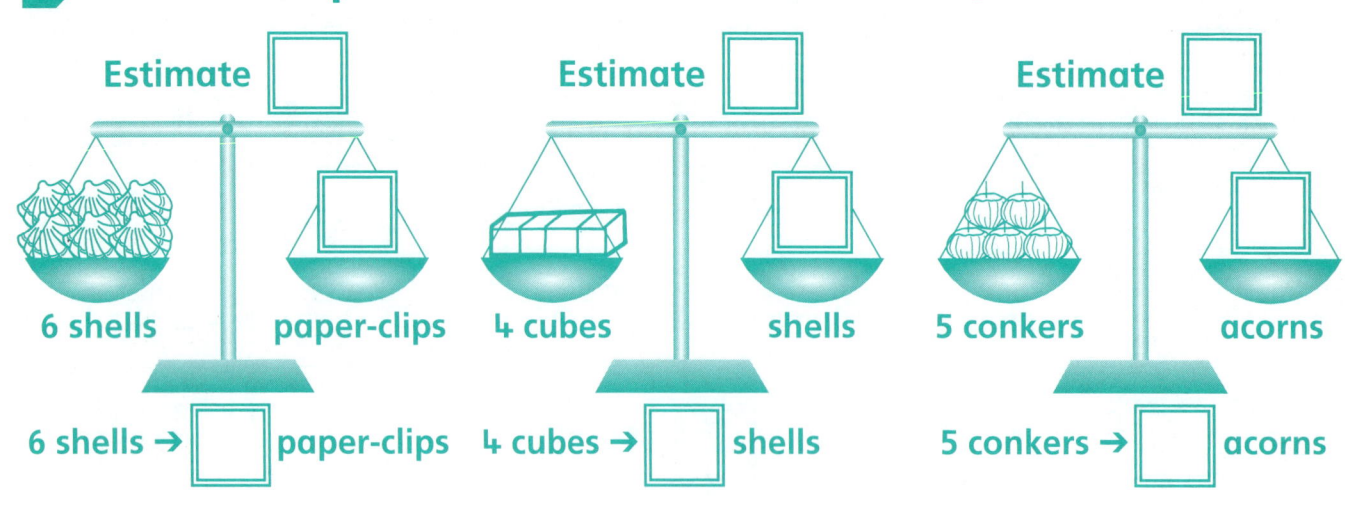

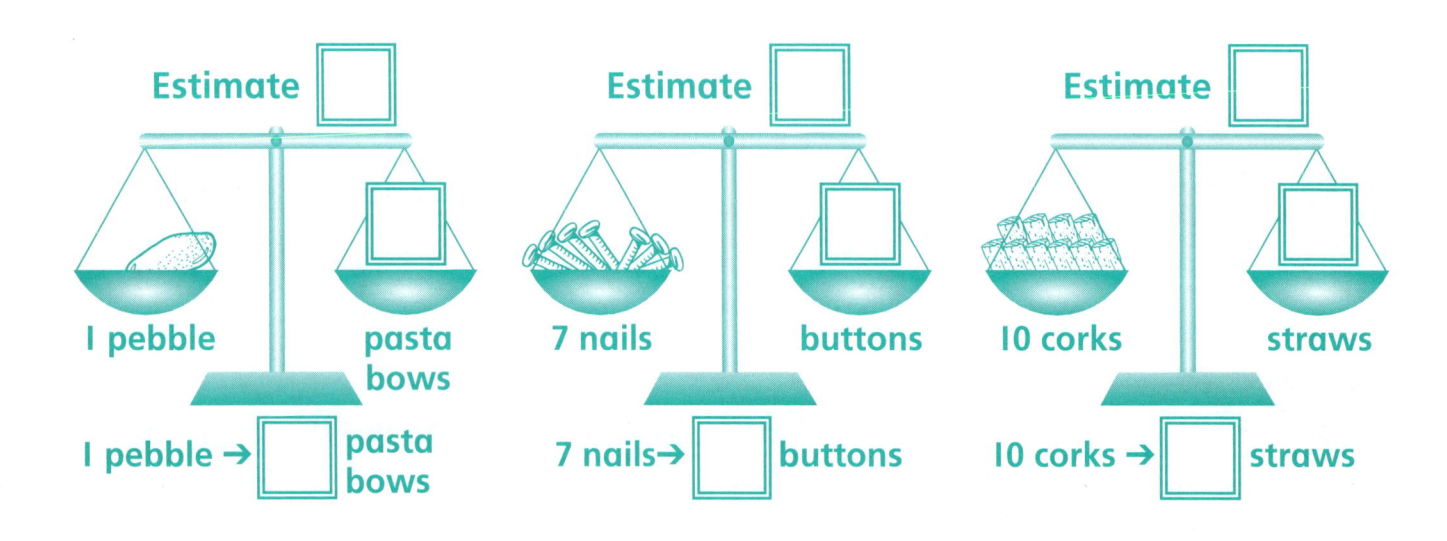

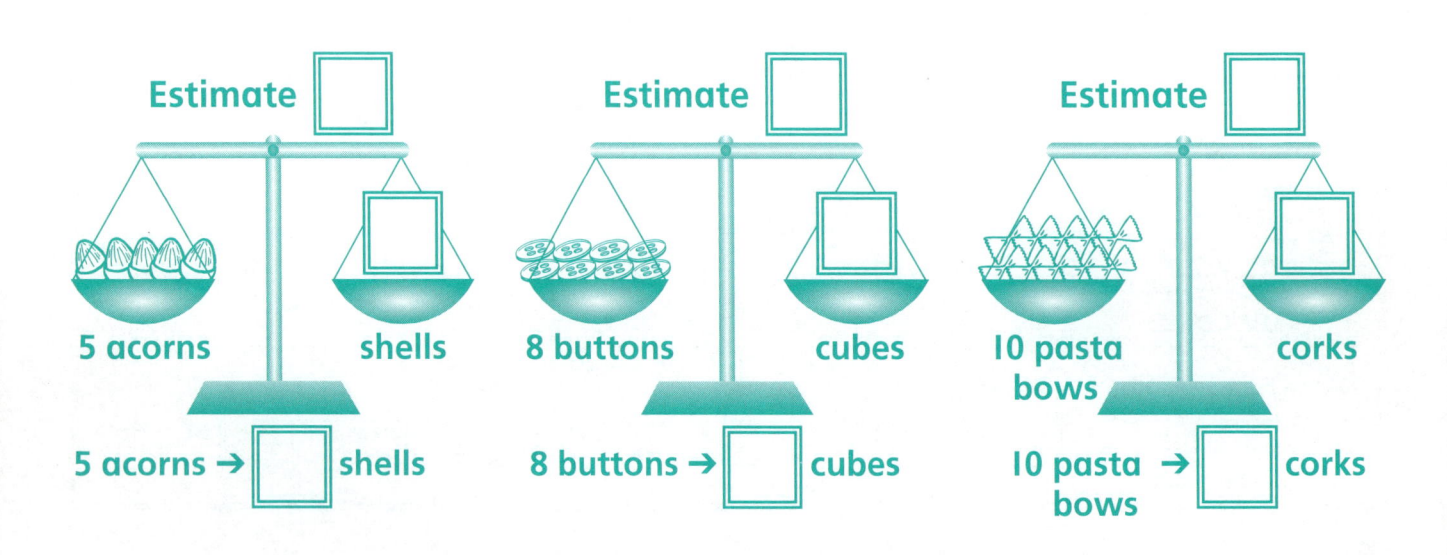

Estimate ☐

6 shells — paper-clips

6 shells → ☐ paper-clips

Estimate ☐

4 cubes — shells

4 cubes → ☐ shells

Estimate ☐

5 conkers — acorns

5 conkers → ☐ acorns

Estimate ☐

1 pebble — pasta bows

1 pebble → ☐ pasta bows

Estimate ☐

7 nails — buttons

7 nails → ☐ buttons

Estimate ☐

10 corks — straws

10 corks → ☐ straws

Estimate ☐

5 acorns — shells

5 acorns → ☐ shells

Estimate ☐

8 buttons — cubes

8 buttons → ☐ cubes

Estimate ☐

10 pasta bows — corks

10 pasta bows → ☐ corks

Turning shapes

▶ **Make a square of a similar size. Match it. Turn it once. Draw round it. Turn it again. Draw round it.**

▶ **Make a rectangle of a similar size. Match it. Turn it once. Draw round it. Turn it again. Draw round it.**

▶ **Make a semicircle of a similar size. Match it. Turn it once. Draw round it. Turn it again. Draw round it.**

▶ **Make a triangle of a similar size. Match it. Turn it once. Draw round it. Turn it again. Draw round it.**

▶ **Make a quarter of a circle of a similar size. Match it. Turn it once. Draw round it. Turn it again. Draw round it.**

Turning shapes

▶ Trace these shapes. Cut them out. Turn them once.
Draw round them. Turn them again. Draw round them.

V

C

L

E

T

Patterns

▶ Finish these patterns.

ee oo ee

no on

▶ Make your own letter pattern here.

▶ Make a word pattern here using "net" and "ten".

▶ Make a pattern here using words and numbers.

two 4 six

▶ Make your own patterns here.

A day at the Fair

PRICE LIST

Big Wheel	8p
Helter-skelter	5p
Ghost Train	9p
Coconut Shy	6p
Roll-a-penny	2p
Big Dipper	7p
Hoop-la	3p
Roundabout	3p
Candy Floss	1p

▶ **What do they cost?**

[6p] [1p]
Coconut Shy and Candy Floss → [7p]

[ ] [ ]
Big Dipper and Roll-a-penny → [ ]

[ ] [ ]
Roundabout and Hoop-la → [ ]

[ ] [ ]
Ghost Train and Candy Floss → [ ]

▶ **How much change?**

Show the change from 10p
(2p) (1p) [ ]p

Show the change from 10p
[ ]p

Show the change from 10p
[ ]p

Show the change from 10p
[ ]p

▶ **Spend 8p on two things:** [ ]

and [ ]

Grand Sale

▶ Take 1p off everything.

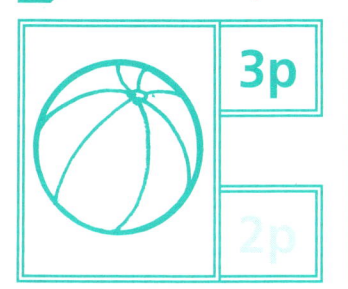

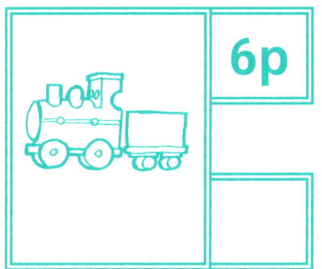

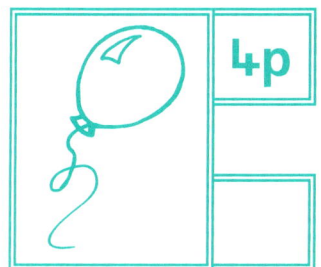

3p	6p	8p	4p
2p			

▶ Take 3p off everything.

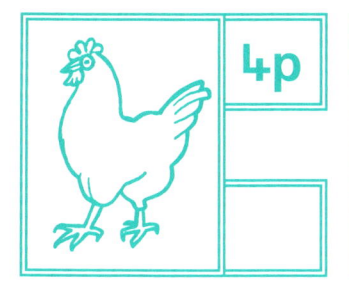

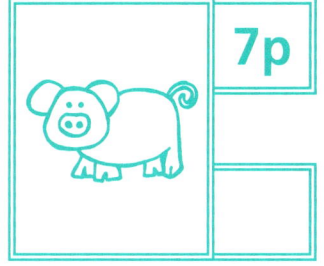

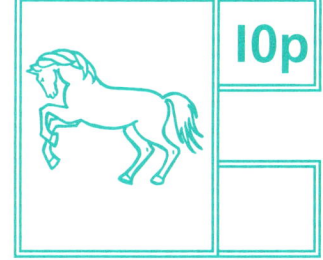

4p	7p	8p	10p

▶ Take 5p off everything.

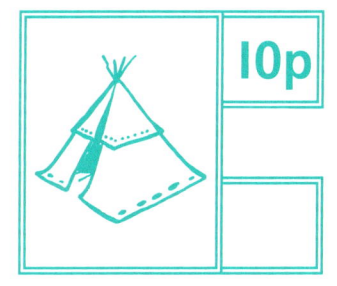

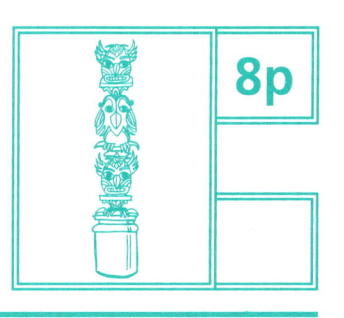

9p	6p	10p	8p

▶ Spend 4p out of each money box.

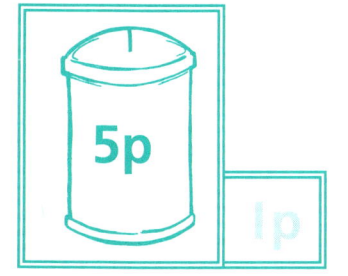

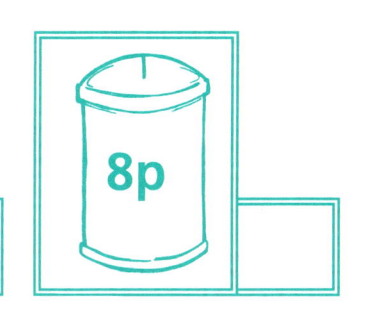

5p	9p	6p	8p
1p			

▶ Spend 2p out of each purse.

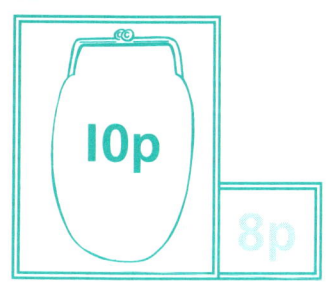

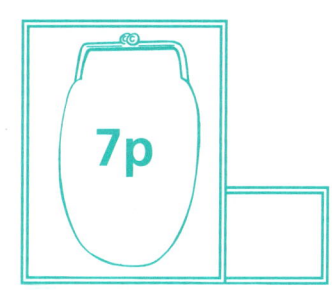

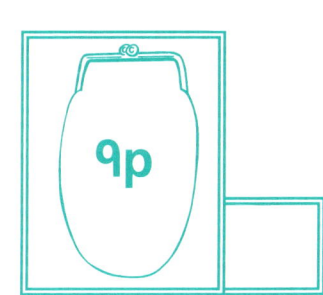

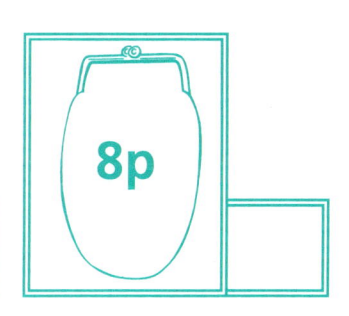

10p	7p	9p	8p
8p			

How many more?

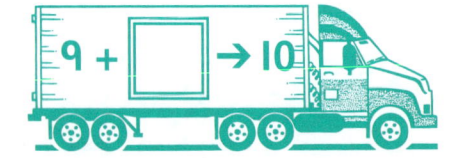

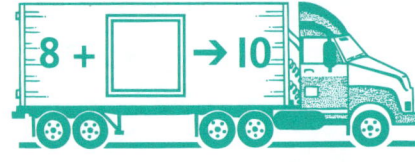

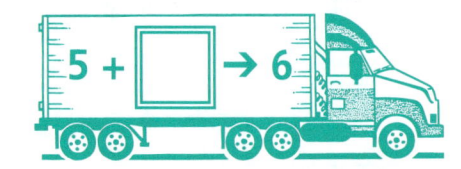

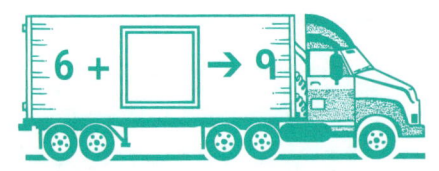

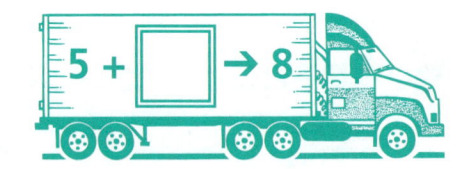

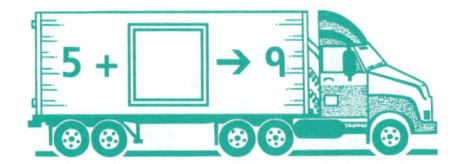

3 + [2] → 5   4 + [ ] → 6   2 + [ ] → 4
3 + [ ] → 6   4 + [ ] → 10   2 + [ ] → 6
3 + [ ] → 7   4 + [ ] → 5   2 + [ ] → 3
3 + [ ] → 9   4 + [ ] → 8   2 + [ ] → 8
3 + [ ] → 4   4 + [ ] → 7   2 + [ ] → 5
3 + [ ] → 8   4 + [ ] → 9   2 + [ ] → 7

6 + [ ] → 8   5 + [ ] → 7   9 + [ ] → 10
7 + [ ] → 9   8 + [ ] → 10   5 + [ ] → 6
5 + [ ] → 10   6 + [ ] → 9   5 + [ ] → 8
6 + [ ] → 7   7 + [ ] → 10   5 + [ ] → 9

▶ 1 more than

7 → [ ]   5 → [ ]   9 → [ ]   6 → [ ]   8 → [ ]

▶ 2 more than

3 → [ ]   8 → [ ]   1 → [ ]   4 → [ ]   0 → [ ]

Our Favourite Pets

▶ Ask 8 children to choose their favourite pet.
Colour a square for their favourite pet.

	dogs	cats	fish	mice	gerbils	rabbits
8						
7						
6						
5						
4						
3						
2						
1						

▶ How many children liked fish best? ☐

▶ How many children liked mice best? ☐

▶ How many children liked cats best? ☐

▶ How many children liked rabbits best? ☐

▶ How many children liked dogs best? ☐

▶ How many children liked gerbils best? ☐

▶ Which pet was the most favourite? _____

▶ Which pet was the least favourite? _____

Key Maths

Titles available: Books 1–5

Graded maths activities for Key Stage 1

Other series from Schofield & Sims Ltd:

	Maths & Science		Language & Literacy	
Early Learning	Workbooks:	Nursery Activity Books	Workbooks:	Early Writing Books, Nursery Activity Books, Nursery Writing Books
Key Stage 1	Workbooks:	Key Maths Number Books	Workbooks:	Basic Skills, First Phonics, Sound Practice
			Readers:	Play Words, Read with the Riddlers, Read and Colour
			Dictionaries:	My Picture Dictionary, My First Picture Dictionary
			Word books:	Picture Words, Early Words, Topic Words
			Copymasters:	Reading Comprehension KS 1
Bridging Key Stages 1 & 2	Workbooks:	Starting Science, Times Tables	Workbooks:	Early Spellings
	Programmes:	Maths Quest	Programmes:	Journeys in Reading, Oracy, Study Reading
	Games:	Master Pieces	Dictionaries:	Illustrated Dictionary, Bilingual Dictionaries
			Word books:	First Words, Early Words
			Copymasters:	Reading Comprehension Bridging Pack
			Games:	Master Pieces
Key Stage 2	Workbooks:	Mental Arithmetic, Homework, Progress Papers – Maths, Times Tables	Workbooks:	Springboard, Spellaway, Key Spellings, Homework, Spelling Practice, Progress Papers – English, Progress Papers – Reasoning
	Practice:	Number Practice, Alpha/Beta, More Practice	Programmes:	English Skills
	Assessment:	Assessment Papers in Maths, Assessment Papers in Science, Practice SATs – Maths	Dictionaries:	Keyword Dictionary, Easy Dictionary, Concise Junior Dictionary, Basic Dictionary, Compact Dictionary, Simplified Dictionary, Spelling Dictionary
			Word books:	Better Words, In Other Words, Choose Your Words, Use Your Words, Classified Spelling
			Assessments:	Assessment Papers in English, Practice SATs – Explorers, Practice SATs – Bicycles
			Copymasters:	Reading Comprehension KS 2, English Practice, Big on Books – Guided Activities for KS 2 Literacy Hour

Schofield & Sims Ltd, Huddersfield, England
Tel: 01484 607080 Fax: 01484 606815

ISBN 0-7217-2455-8

9 780721 724553